Real Estate Deal Or No Deal

How To Tell When You Have A Deal Or Not

By

Ernie Braveboy

Get Your Free Copy of

How to be a Real Estate Millionaire

To Get Your Free Copy, Open the Link

https://ebraveboy_3ee2.gr8.com/

© **Copyright 2018 Ernie Braveboy - All rights reserved.**

This document is geared towards providing exact and reliable information in regards to the topic and issue covered. The publication is sold with the idea that the publisher is not required to render the accounting, officially permitted, or otherwise, qualified services. If advice is necessary, legal or professional, a practiced individual in the profession should be ordered.

- From a Declaration of Principles which was accepted and approved equally by a Committee of the American Bar Association and a Committee of Publishers and Associations.

In no way is it legal to reproduce, duplicate, or transmit any part of this document in either electronic means or in printed format. Recording of this publication is strictly prohibited and any storage of this document is not allowed unless with written permission from the publisher. All rights reserved.

The information provided herein is stated to be truthful and consistent, in that any liability, in terms of inattention or otherwise, by any usage or abuse of any policies, processes, or directions contained within is the solitary and utter responsibility of the recipient reader. Under no circumstances will any legal responsibility or blame be held against the publisher for any reparation, damages, or monetary loss due to the information herein, either directly or indirectly.

Respective authors own all copyrights not held by the publisher.

The information herein is offered for informational purposes solely and is universal as so. The presentation of the information is without a contract or any type of guarantee assurance.

The trademarks that are used are without any consent, and the publication of the trademark is without permission or backing by the trademark owner. All trademarks and brands within this book are for clarifying purposes only and are the owned by the owners themselves, not affiliated with this document.

INTRODUCTION

I want to thank you and congratulate you for buying the book, *"Real Estate Deal Or No Deal: How To Tell When You Have A Deal Or Not"*.

This book will give you actionable information on how to determine whether any real estate deal that you come across is worth taking or not.

As a real estate investor or a person looking to buy a property, you will constantly get deals from brokers. The question you may always have to ask yourself is; how are you supposed to know if the deals you are getting are good and worth pursuing? And the truth is, that is one of the hardest things to figure out as a real estate investor. But that shouldn't worry you because this book is going to teach you how to tell when you have a deal or not.

This guide is first going to teach you the basics of real estate investing and then from there take you through a step by step process that will help you determine when a real estate deal is viable. Some of the topics that will be discussed in this book include;

- What's so special about real estate?

- What is real estate and what are the common terms used in real estate

- What is the definition of a great real estate deal?

- What should you look for when searching for a property?

- Step by step process on how to determine when a real estate deal is viable.

By the end of this book, you will not just have learned the basics of real estate that will lay a great foundation for any future deals you might have but you will have also learned how to tell when you have a great real estate deal so that you take it before anyone else does.

This guide is simply going to drive you towards your next real estate deal and place you on a steady path to success.

Let's start.

Thanks again for buying this book. I hope you enjoy it!

TABLE OF CONTENTS

Real Estate Deal Or No Deal 1

   How To Tell When You Have A Deal Or Not 1

Introduction v

Basic Education Of Real Estate Investing 5

   Real Estate Terms 5

   Real Estate Mathematics 7

   Define A Great Deal 9

   Real Estate Strategy 11

How Are You Supposed To Find Deals In Real Estate? 19

   Approach 1: Finding Real Estate Deals Online: How To. 19

   Approach 2: Finding Real Estate in Person 21

Evaluating Cash Flow Investing Deals 23

   Financial Analysis 23

   Step 1: Calculate Net Operating Income (NOI) 30

      Assess the Property Expenses 34

      Calculate Net Operating Income 35

   Step 2: Calculating Your Cash Flow 36

   Step 3: Find Out Your Rate Of Return 39

   Cash-On-cash Return (COC) 42

Total ROI 43
Evaluating A Real Estate Wholesaling Deal 45
    Step 1: Gather Information 46
    Step 2: Do Some Wholesaling Mathematics 50
    How To Come Up With The ARV 52
Evaluating Real Estate Rehabbing Deal 56
    Step 1: Learn How To Identify A Good House To Flip 56
    Step 2: Determine the ARV (After Repaired Value) 60
    Step 3: Approximate The Repair Cost 62
    Step 4: Calculate the Holding and Closing Expenses 63
    Step 5: Determine Your Profit Expectation 66
    Step 7: Calculate Your Offer 66
Conclusion 68

What's So Special About Real Estate?

Real estate investing is basically the purchase, lease, ownership or sale of land with an aim of earning an income. But why invest in real estate? What's so special about it?

Today, there are a lot of places that you can invest your money in which include mutual funds, bonds, stocks, currencies, savings, and commodities. But one of the best places for you to invest your money and time it is in real estate. A lot of us consider it an 'alternative asset' because they think of it as a hard nut to crack kind of investment but that's not true. Real estate is a lucrative and dependable way of generating income and any one of us can succeed in it by learning how to spot the right deal which is what this book is going to teach you.

So back to our question, why invest in real estate? Below are some of the reasons why:

1. It has a hedge against inflation

Traditional investments like mutual funds, bonds and stocks are usually highly affected by inflation. That is why investors of these investments consider how compounded or constant inflation is when investing. Even if their investments rise in value over time, they still consider the inflation rate because if their investments don't keep up with the inflation rate, they will lose money. For instance, if the annual inflation rate is 2% and your investment is 1% per year then you will be losing money.

One of the reasons why real estate investing is so special and important is because it does not get affected by inflation. Why? This is because property normally reacts in proportion to inflation. Whenever inflation rises, home prices and rent also rise. So there is no day inflation will affect your investment, as it is always in step with or ahead of market values and trends.

2. It has amazing tax benefits

Real estate investing is an attractive investment because it attracts a lot of tax exemptions when you own a property either as an owner or just an investor. For instance, the government offers tax breaks for property taxes, legal fees, travel expenses, maintenance repairs, insurance, and property depreciation. But that's not all when you own your property, the rental income is usually not subjected to self-employment tax. As an investor, you are entitled to lower taxes rates for your long-term investment. Those are a lot of tax exemption goodies for anyone who invests in real estate.

3. It is a high tangible asset value

One of the reasons why investing in real estate is such a good idea is because the property is always a valuable asset, with an ever-increasing value. This is unique because it does not always happen in other investment fields. For instance, a stock can deep to zero at any time and other investments like your car constantly decrease in value as time passes by. As you can see, real estate is the only investment that always holds value to you.

4. It has a steady income

One of the obvious reasons why real estate is so special is because of its ability to give you a steady income, especially rental income if you are investing in rental property.

Real estate gives you an opportunity to receive a flow of cash over long-term. But that's not even the good part. The good part is, there is no limit to your return on real estate. You can get 10 %, 15%, 20% or even more of the money you have invested per year.

5. It has a high leverage

Another huge advantage of real estate investment is its power of leverage, especially if you are looking to invest your own money. In real estate investing, you are allowed to put down a small percentage of a property's market price/value and own the investment in full. In fact, real estate is the only investment plan where you can put down just $40k and own a property worth $130k. This is unique because it is impossible for you to enter into a bank and offer to give them $2000 in exchange for $10,000 in stocks.

As you can see, real estate investing is a productive and profitable business and one that is worth pursuing. But for you to be successful in it, you not only need to know how to tell when you have a deal, you also need to have a full understanding of what the field of real estate is all about. Learn that in the chapter below.

ERNIE BRAVEBOY

BASIC EDUCATION OF REAL ESTATE INVESTING

While real estate is good at helping you create a consistent income stream, it can seem intimidating if you don't know what you are doing. That's where this chapter comes in. This chapter is going to educate you on the basics of real estate investment that will help you have an easier time during your search and purchase of real estate. In this chapter, you are going to learn real estate terms, real estate mathematics, how to define a great deal and the strategies that you can use to make money in real estate. Let's get on with it;

Real Estate Terms

As a home buyer or a real estate investor, you will surely come across all sorts of real estate terminology that real estate professionals use amongst themselves. These terminologies are very important for you to learn because if you don't, you will be creating a language barrier hurdle for yourself; and that's the last thing you want when you are a real estate investor.

Here are some of the essential terminologies that you need to learn their meaning.

- ✓ Operating expenses -This is the collective expenditure that you incur when keeping a property in service or operational. Some of these costs include routine maintenance, utilities, insurance, and property taxes.

- ✓ Listing -This term is used to refer to homes that are on sale.

- ✓ Inspection:-Once you make an offer on a home, you are required to schedule an inspection where an inspector comes in and inspects the home.

- ✓ Contingencies- Contingencies are the conditions that must be met before you, the buyer, can complete a deal from an offer.

- ✓ Appraisal- This is an estimated property value that has been determined by a qualified appraiser.

- ✓ Down payment- This is the amount that you pay towards a property purchase before your lender gives you a loan to stand for the rest of the purchase amount. It is normally 3-20percent of the total cost.

- ✓ Title- This is the legal term and document that shows a piece of property is lawfully processed by an owner.

- ✓ Realtors- They are real estate agents that are members of the National Association of Realtors.

- ✓ Multiple Listing Service (MLS)- This is a large database that shows detailed information on properties that are currently under contract on the market or sold.

- ✓ Equity- It refers to the difference between a property's fair market value and the unsettled balanced of the mortgage; for instance, if your home is worth 500,000 and you owe 200,000, your equity is 300,000.

- ✓ Mortgage- This is a loan that banks give buyers of real estate properties to buy the property.
- ✓ Earnest money deposit- This is the money that accompanies a buyers offer on a property to show good faith. If the offer goes through the amount is used in your down payment. If your offer is rejected, the amount is returned to you.

Those are the basic technologies that you are going to come across when you get into real estate. The second thing that you must learn is real estate mathematics.

Real Estate Mathematics

Here are some of the basic math formulas you will need to understand when you want to buy a property.

Income- This is simply the amount of money that you get from a property. This amount usually includes the rent of the house and any additional fees like fees for using the garage, vending machine, laundry, pet, application fees, and late fees. For instance, if your house earns you $500 rent and the tenant pays $50 for using the vending machine & $10 for using the garage, your income will be 500+50+50=500

Expenses

Expenses are basically the costs that you incur on an investment. These costs include the bank loan interest, maintenance fee, taxes, capital expenses, holding cost and insurance cost among others. To get the expenses of a property, you need to add all the expenses. For instance, if the bank loan per month is $200, the electricity bill is $50, garbage bill is $50, insurance cost is $100 and maintenance cost is $130 then your total expenses will be 200+50+50+100+130=520

ROI (Return on investment)

This stands for the interest rate that you make on your money per year. For instance, if your money is $300 and you made $300 from the investment, you will have made a 100% return on investment. If you invest $4,000 and made $2,000 from your investment, you would have made a 50% return on investment.

Cash flow

Cash flow is basically the amount you get as a property owner at the end of the month after you have paid all expenses. To get your cash flow, you need to subtract total expenses from your total income. For instance, if your income was $2,000 and expenses $500, your cash flow will be $1,500.

Now that you have been enlightened on the commonly used words in RE, you are ready to get into real estate investing as either a home buyer or an investor.

Now for you to learn how to tell when you have a deal or not, you must first identify what the right deal is for you. Read on to learn how.

Define A Great Deal

Every person who goes to buy a house or invest in real estate develop their own opinion of what a good deal is. Basically, what we are saying is that there is no one size fits all solutions when it comes to the right deal.

What I mean by this is that a property can be a great deal to you but a mediocre and a poor deal for the next person. Therefore, you need to identify your best deal depending on your situation. But how should you do that?

It's simple; you need to identify 2 things,

- Your objective
- The real estate strategy that you want to venture into

Your objective in investing in real estate

Each one of us gets into real estate because of a reason. To know what a great real estate deal is to you, you need to find out what that reason is for you. For instance, if your dream has always been to buy a nice house then your reason for entering real estate might be to find a perfect house that you can call home.

On the other hand, commercial real estate investors normally have a wide range of objectives that makes them want to invest in real estate. Below are a couple of objectives that you can have as a commercial real estate investor:

- To build wealth that you can use for retirement

- For inflation protection

- For getting regular cash flow

- For generating profit

- As an investment portfolio diversification

For you to know the purpose or the objective of getting into real estate, you must ask yourself; what makes you want to take part in real estate? Is it the money that you hope to make; is it your desire to get a house of your own or is it because you want to create another source of income? Whatever the answer is, that is your objective. That said, a good objective is the one that is precise and detailed. To make your real estate more detailed, you need to use the SMART formulae.

Here is how this formula makes you make a goal/objective that is –

S- Specific

M- Measurable

A- Attainable

R-Relevant

T-Time bond

A good example of a detailed objective for doing real estate is; I want to get into real estate in order to buy two properties which will earn me about $500 each month before the end of this year.

Real Estate Strategy

Now that you have discovered your goal, the next step is for you to look at and decide which real estate strategy of making money you will be comfortable using to achieve your goal.

Below are the three core strategies of real estate investing.

1. **Real estate wholesaling**

Real estate wholesaling is one of the tried and true strategies of generating cash in real estate. What you are required to do in wholesaling is to find great deals (properties that are being sold for less than their worth either because the seller is in a certain urgency to sell the property or the house is in bad condition among many other things), write a contract to acquire the deal and then sell the contract to another buyer for a profit.

In this method, you don't get to own the property; you instead put the property under contract and sell the contract to another buyer.

You make money in this method by earning the difference between what the contract price was and what the end buyer agreed to pay for it. For instance, you can get a $150,000 worth property under contract and sell it to the end buyer at $160,000. This means you will have earned $10,000.

As a wholesaler, you can get paid in days or weeks, which makes this strategy an easy one as it also has a low start-up cost. Most real estate investors start with this strategy and it is advisable for you to start with this strategy too if you are new to real estate investing.

2. Real estate rehabbing

Real estate rehabbing or flipping, as it's commonly known, is one of the most popular strategies of making money in real estate. Real estate rehabbing is basically buying an investment property at a discounted price (which is mostly broken down or beat up) then make a major or a minor improvement to it before reselling it for a higher price.

One of the vital aspects of house flipping is speed. As a flipper, you need to be as quick as you can in rehabbing and selling a house you have just bought. This is because of speed guarantees maximum profitability, as it saves you from the carrying monthly costs such as maintenance bills, utility bills, condo fees, property taxes, and other financial bills. ☐

3. Cash flow investing

The third strategy that you can use to make a profit in real estate is cash flow investing which is also known as the buy and hold strategy. This strategy involves you buying a property and renting it out to receive on-going cash flow. It is probably the simplest form of real estate investing. A cash flow real estate investor can create wealth by renting the property out and also by holding the property and selling the property for a good gain in the future. The advantage with this method is that you can do both i.e. rent the property out with plans of selling it in the future; which is a very lucrative deal because the renting the house out will help you pay off your mortgage as it increases your equity in the property.

So how can you find a good deal in real estate? Learn that in the chapter below.

How To Find A Good Real Estate Deal

The truth is, it is very hard to find a great real estate deal. But to tell whether a real estate deal is worth it or not, you need to first find one; and this chapter is going to help you do that. Before you can see how to find a good real estate deal, it is important for you to know why a lot of people don't find good investment properties. The reason is that we look at investment deals all wrong. How? It is funny but the things that we actually think are making us successful in real estate are actually the ones that make us fail to get a great real estate deal. Below are some of the wrong things that we do.

1. Being a jack of all trades

As you now know, real estate is a lucrative venture that can make you a lot of money and the good thing about it is that there are numerous strategies that you can use to make that money. For instance, you can rent out a property, flip a property and wholesale or invest in residential and commercial houses. One of the mistakes that make us fail to succeed in finding a great deal is the feeling of wanting to make money using all the real estate strategies. In short being a jack of all trades.

But why is that wrong? It's wrong because when you are open to using all strategies, you are attracted by every deal that comes your way. This then makes you find yourself in a wild goose chase because you will see a house flipping opportunity, look at it and just when you are about to analyze it, you see another deal that is more attractive but this time is in the rent and hold strategy. That trend then goes on for weeks if not months, which makes it so difficult for you to get a deal and concentrate on it to a point where you discover it's a great deal.

That is one thing that can hold you back. You can overcome it by doing what you learned earlier in this book, which is to pick one strategy, do a proper business plan on it and go with it. When you have a harmer, you only look for a nail. So lock yourself down to only one option so that you can find yourself a great deal.

2. You are reading too much about real estate

Another reason that holds you back from finding a deal and a great one for that matter is believing that for you to start looking for a real estate deal, you must read and know everything about real estate. Yes, it is important for you to have some knowledge about real estate before getting into it but that mentality normally diverts your attention from being a real estate investor to being a full-time scholar of real estate. This is usually a wrong way of looking at real estate because of two things:

- ✓ Gaining all the knowledge about real estate is useless if you do not use it to put a great real estate deal together.
- ✓ You don't have to read a lot and become an expert for you to start closing some deals. You just have to be

good enough and have the courage to start finding deals.

3. Treating real estate as a side gig

Treating real estate as a side gig is another mentality and way of looking at real estate that drags you behind as a real estate investor that needs to be able to strike the best deals.

Why is this mentality destructive? As you saw above, real estate is a path to wealth. It is a channel that has made a lot of people millionaires and a channel that many uses as their only source of income. However, there is a catch for real estate to be as lucrative; it needs you to concentrate on it. In short, it needs a lot of attention.

However, this doesn't mean you cannot do other jobs when doing real estate; it just means you will need to concentrate on real estate more than you would when you think of it as a side gig because thinking of it as a side gig means you will only concentrate on real estate when all your work is through. For instance, you can have an 8 a.m - 5 p.m office job and still do real estate. All you have to do is to create spaces when you can concentrate on real estate. For example, on your tea break, you can look at some real estate deals online, when driving home, you can be checking out properties for sale and when talking to your colleges and friends, you can be telling them about you being a real estate investor. Moreover, thinking like a real estate investor much of the time will also undoubtedly help you find deals with greater ease, as you will be always alert to investing opportunities.

At this point, it is okay if you still are wondering how exactly you will hunt for great deals in real estate. That's what we will be discussing next.

How Are You Supposed To Find Deals In Real Estate?

One of the keys to investing in property as a home buyer or a real estate investor is to find good deals and close them before someone else grabs them. The question now is; how can you find real estate deal that you can analyze to determine whether they are good or not? Well, you can use either of the 2 methods to find real estate deals. One is finding deals online and the other one is finding deals in person. Below are a breakdown and explanation of the two methods.

Approach 1: Finding Real Estate Deals Online: How To

The internet is perhaps the first place you should check out if you are looking for real estate properties that are on sale. The good thing is that there are different approaches to finding good properties online.

1: MLS (Multiple Listing Service) and similar portals

The MLS is a popular online database where sellers list their real estate properties for sale. If a real estate property is on sale, you will probably get it on MLS. That's how popular it is. As a property hunter, therefore, the MLS is one of the best places to go find real estate deals. It is especially important to check out the local Multiple Listing Service, as it usually aggregates information that realtors and licensed real estate professionals rely on so you can be sure that what you find here is legit. It is so comprehensive that most websites pull information from local MLS to list properties in different areas. As a beginner, it is best to use a real estate agent or broker.

Other websites where you can find real estate properties that are on sale include:

- Zillow.com
- Trulia.com
- HomeFinder.com
- Homes.com
- Redfin.com
- Auction.com
- HomeSales.gov

2: LoopNet

LoopNet is one of the best online real estate marketplaces. As of 2012, LoopNet had more than 8 million members. LoopNet is mainly for larger residential and commercial properties. So if that falls under your niche, you can look for them there.

3: FSBO (for sale by owner)

FSBO is another online resource that you can use when searching for a real estate deal. In FSBO, a seller is allowed to list his/her property where potential buyers like you can view and buy properties. A good example of FSBO sites includes Craigslist, Redfin, owners.com, and FSBO.com.

The good thing about searching for real estate properties online is that you get to have a feel for what the market has to offer in a given location. You will know when a price is out of the prevailing market rate in a given area so that you can be more careful to know what warrants a premium price. That way, even if you start checking out local properties in person, you know for sure what the typical buyer will be looking for in a given area.☐

Approach 2: Finding Real Estate in Person

The second way of finding real estate deals is in person. You can use different approaches to go about it. Let's discuss some of these ways next.

1: Word Of Mouth

Real estate investing is a people business. This means anyone you come across from your mailman, friend and family have the potential to lead you to a real estate deal as well as being a potential investor in your property. Therefore, one of the most effective ways through which you can find real estate deals, especially the off the market deals, is by marketing yourself through word of mouth. You can do this by telling everyone you interact with about the fact that you are actively looking for real estate deals.

2: Public Record

Public records like newspapers and government websites occasionally inform the public about real estate properties that are about to be listed. This is another place that you can look into and find a great deal. The public record can also mention foreclosed and pre-foreclosure properties, which also provide you with an opportunity to find a great real estate deal.

3: Knocking On People's Doors

Many times, people get into a situation where they can't manage their houses anymore and need to sell them. Such deals are usually off the market and the only way you can get them is to knock on doors in search for these deals. Of course, you cannot knock on everyone's door but you can look for distressed looking properties and approach them as a potential investor or house buyer.

Now you know how to scout for real estate deals. Unfortunately, most real estate deals are not great investments. The chapter below is going to educate you on how to tell a great real estate deal.

EVALUATING CASH FLOW INVESTING DEALS

The previous chapter has taught you the different ways you can use to find real estate deals. By following the above methods, you will definitely get all kinds of real estate deals and your work will be to now analyze them and see if they are worth your time and money. In this section, you are going to be taught how to go about figuring out whether a cash flow property that you are supposed to rent out is a good deal or a total rip off?

To know if a rental property that you might be considering buying is worth it, you will need to do a thorough financial analysis.

Financial Analysis

What you are about to learn is how to analyze different sized multi-unit residential property and single-family rentals. That said, the value for single-family homes is determined differently from multi-family properties.

Let me explain.

The market value of single-family houses, whether they are investments or not, are usually determined by the comparable houses that are in the same area and have similar characteristics (like having the same number of bathrooms and bedrooms, the same type of floor plan, garage size and other amenities). This means that the value of a single house rises and lowers in value when it's neighboring houses that are similar to it rise and lower in value.

Multi-family properties and large investment properties are valued and priced differently from the single-family houses. This is because the value of large properties is determined by how much profit or income it produces for its owner. This goes to show you just how important good financial analysis is when you want to find out whether a property is a good deal or not.

Here is a step by step process of analyzing a rental property.

Step 1: Gather property details

The first step to analyzing how viable a rental property is is to gather the property details. By 'property details', I mean the information about the physical design of rental houses, which include the number of utility metering design, square footage and a number of units. You are supposed to get this information from the seller of the property but you can also find a more comprehensive and elaborate information of the same from your local county records.

Step 2: Get the purchase information

The second step you should take is to get all the purchase information of the property you are considering buying. The purchase information normally consists of the basic cost information of the property. One of the basic cost information includes the purchase price of the property improvement or rehab costs. This information is usually given to you by the seller of the property.

That said, you should never rely only on the information given to you by the seller; you should also have the property inspected so that you can get actual data on the property.

But why go through all that trouble?

Well, when it comes to purchasing information, it's in the seller's best interest if he/she can give out information that appeals to you as opposed to the accurate information. For instance, a seller can easily lie about the rental income potential of the property or omit important information about the property like it's maintenance cost.

That is why you shouldn't solely rely on the information given to you by the seller. You should instead make sure you carry out private inspection and get the appropriate information before closing on the deal. If need be, you can ask to see maintenance records, property tax bills and his/her previous year's tax returns, which can help you come up with the right information. The point here is to make sure you don't get any surprises when you buy the property.

Step 3: Get your financial details

Now that you have all this information, you can now go ahead and find a way of financing the deal. For most investors, they get their funding from the banks. If you have to apply for a loan as well, this is the step where you gather all the information about your financial position and any relevant information to ensure that if you want to close, you won't experience any ugly surprises. This includes the total loan amount, closing costs, interest rate, and down payment amount among other things.

Step 4: Find out about the income

The 4th step is for you to find out the detailed information about the income that the property you want produces. This information is very important because it helps you determine the amount of return the property will give you. That then helps you in analyzing if the property is a good deal or not.

The income the property produces is information that you get from the seller. However, as we mentioned earlier, you should never rely on pro-forma data for your final analysis. You should always find more accurate information. For instance, you can ask for income information from the property management company if the property has one. That way, you will get a more detailed information.

Step 5: Find out about the expenses

One of the most important details to collect when it comes to property analysis is getting detailed information about the expenses of the property. This information gives you a good idea of what you are going to spend on it. That is usually crucial information when trying to figure out whether the property is profitable or not.

Just like income details, you should never fully trust the seller's information. You should do your own investigations to get information that you can actually rely on. You will get this information from the property management company if there is one for the property. You can also use a building inspector who can give you information that is more accurate. The expense information that you are supposed to get includes the cost of maintaining the property like maintenance costs, insurance, and property taxes.

The above are the five factors you must take into account when analyzing a property and I cannot stress enough how it is your responsibility to do your own due diligence of gathering information when you want to buy property that you want to rent out. Now we are going to look at a real-life real estate deal and how you are supposed to implement the five factors to figure out if the real estate property is a good deal or not.

Here are the high- level details of an apartment building that is up for sale.

10-unit complex (2 Duplexes) in a quiet neighborhood outside of town

Primary Type: Multi-Family residential garden- style low rise

No of units: 4

Price: $500,000

Cap Rate: 9%

Year built: 1970

Lot size: 44 Acres

Property description

This 10-unit complex is all brick in downtown Melville neighborhood. A mix of units with front and back entrances, townhome floor plans and hardwood floors. The property has 9 residents and only one vacancy. The vacant unit has some damages that will require about $10,000 in repairs before it becomes good for leasing.

Financial Summary Pro-Forma	Unit Mix/Rent
Year 2010	5 1BR+1BT/ $540
Gross Income $54,000	3 1BR+ 1BT/ $580
Other Income (Laundry) $2,400	2 2BR+ 1BT/ $670
Vacancy 12%	
Expenses	
Taxes $5,000	
Insurance $800	
Maintenance $3,500	
Advertising $300	
Utilities $2,000	

One of the information that is missing from the high-level detail of the above apartment building is your financial details. That's because that kind of detail comes from you, the potential buyer, and not the seller. Your financial details are usually between you and your mortgage broker or lender. For the sake of this example, we are going to assume you talked to your bank or with whoever your lender is and you secured a loan that covers the following;

- The price of the property: $500,000

- Improvement cost: $10,000

- Finance amount: 80% of the total cost

- Interest Rate: Fixed 7% over 30 years

- Closing costs: 2% of the total property cost

Now that you have all the above information, your next step is to jump straight into a thorough analysis of the property that will help you know if the property is a good deal or not. Below are the steps that you should take in analyzing the property.

Step 1: Calculate Net Operating Income (NOI)

One of the essential metrics of real estate financial analysis is NOI and this is because it helps you know just how much a particular property generates. NOI is basically the total income that a property generates after you have subtracted all the expenses (excluding loan costs) that the property incurs.

The formulae: *Income- Expenses= NOI*

But why don't we include the loan when calculating the NOI when it is an expense that can affect the bottom line of this analysis? That question will be answered in the next step.

NOI is calculated on a monthly basis meaning you will use the property monthly income and expenses when calculating; after that, you can convert it to an annual analysis by multiplying it by 12.

So how are you supposed to go about calculating the NOI of the above property deal?

Here is how:

Assess the property income

The first thing that you are going to do is to calculate the gross income of the property. Gross income basically means the total income that is generated from the property and this includes income that comes from tenants rent, parking fees, laundry facilities and any other income that the property makes on a monthly basis. Now let's start calculating the gross income of the above property.

Rent

As you saw above, the property has 10 units but only nine of those units are rented out. So how much does this property make in rent per month?

No. of Units	Rent per Unit	Total
5	$540	$2,700
3	$580	$1,740
2	$670	$1,340
TOTAL		**$5,780**

Laundry

The laundry income per month is $200.

Now that you have got the rent income per month, which is $ 5,780 and the laundry income per month, which is $200, you should now convert it into an annual figure.

Rent; 5,780 x 12 months= $69,360

Laundry; 200 x 12 months= $2,400

For your analysis to be accurate, which it needs to be, your income calculation needs to take into account the vacant unit that you were informed about in the property details. This is important because that one vacancy represents rent that you won't be getting. In our property, only one unit was listed as vacant so the vacancy rate is:

- ✓ **1 x100= 100 divides by 10 which is 10%** (vacancy rate is calculated by multiplying the number of vacant units by 100 and dividing the result by total amount of units in a property)

So our monthly income for our property when we consider the vacant unit should be:

Rental income that you won't get per month; 12% of 5,780 = 578

Rental income you will get per month; 5,780 - 578 = 5,202

Rental income per year; 5,202 x 12= 62,424

Gross income; 2,400 (laundry) + 62,424= 64,834

So the correct amount of total annual income that you will get from the 10-unit complex is $64,834 per year.

Assess the Property Expenses

The second thing you are going to do is to calculate the 10-unit complex property expenses. Some of the things that you are going to add in this category include utility expenses (if the expenses are paid by the owner), landscaping expenses, advertising expenses, expenses for hiring a professional property manager, insurance and property taxes.

The expenses for the 10-unit complex property are as follows:

Item	Amount ($)
Property taxes	5000
Insurance	800
Maintenance	3500
Advertising	300
Utilities	2000
Property management 6% of rent	3745
Total	15,345

The total expense listed above has been listed as an annual expense amount. When you calculate expenses, you should always make sure you have converted it into an annual cost.

Calculate Net Operating Income

Now that you have the total annual income and expenses for the property, you can now calculate the NOI. As you saw above, NOI = Income − Expenses. So our NOI should be:

$64,834 − $15,345 = $49,489

The net operating income per year is $49,489. That said, calculating the NOI is just one of the steps that you take towards a full analysis of a property. The NOI only cannot give you the information you need to make a decision on whether a property is worth it or not but it is an important metric in a property analysis.

Step 2: Calculating Your Cash Flow

The previous step raised a very important question that was to be answered later. Well, this is the step that actually answers that question.

So why do we exclude the debt service costs when calculating Net Operating Income? The reason why the loan cost is excluded is that the NOI calculation focuses on coming up with the level of income a property can produce independently of your financial details as an owner.

Let me break it down for you: if you were to include the debt service cost when calculating NOI then you will have an income that is only meaningful to a particular financing plan. This means that each and every investor would have a custom made NOI because we all have different financial plans. By leaving out the debt service cost, the measure of net operating income provides a metric that is specific to the property and not the buyer, which means any owner can use the metrics when analyzing the property.

But isn't the debt service cost an important factor that needs to be factored when analyzing a property? The answer is yes and that's why we have cash flow calculation as our second step. Basically, cash flow is exactly like NOI, only this time, it incorporates the debt service cost as an expense. The formula for finding cash flow is:

NOI – Debt service = Cash flow

If you pay for the property with your own money, then you will not have a debt service costs, which means your cash flow will be the amount that you find when calculating NOI.

So how do you calculate the cash flow of the 10-unit complex property? For you to calculate the cash flow, you must first calculate your monthly debt service.

Here are the calculations that you need to come up with the monthly debt service:

Cost Assumptions	
Purchase price	$500,000
Down-payment	$100,000
Improvements	$10,000
Closing costs	$10,000
Total cost	$520,000
Cash outlay (amount for operating expenses)	$120,000

Financing Assumptions	
Down-payment	20%
Finance amount	$400,000
Down-payment amount	$100,000
Interest rate	7%
Mortgage (Years)	30
Mortgage payment	$2,641

The formula for calculating your monthly debt service cost is:

$A = P[r(1+r)^n] / [(1+r)^n - 1]$

A stands for amount per month

P stands for the principal (loan amount)

R stands for interest rate per period

N stands for the total number of payments

In our case, you will first divide the interest rate by 12 to get the interest rate per period so 7/12= 0.583. Then calculate the total number of monthly payments by *multiplying 30 years with 12 months= 360 months. Now feed the details you have in the formula*

A= 520,00[0.583(1 + 0.583) ^ 360] / [(1 + 0.583) ^ 360 − 1] The answer should be $2,641.

You can also find the monthly debt service cost by using online calculators that will calculate it for you. All you have to do is to feed the information to the calculator. Below are links to good mortgage calculators.

Https://www.nerdwallet.com/mortgages/mortgage-calculator/calculate-mortgage-payment

https://www.scotiabank.com/mortgage/payment/en/payment.html

So now that you have determined the monthly debt service for the 10-unit complex, the next step is for you to convert it to an annual debt service by multiplying it by 12.

2,641 x 12 = $31,692

For this property, our cash flow will be NOI − Debt service, which is 49,489 − 31,692 = 17,797. So for this property, you will have a profit of $17,797 by the end of the year.

Step 3: Find Out Your Rate Of Return

The previous step showed you how much you are going to gain at the end of the year, which is a very important piece of information to have. But what is more important than that is finding out your rate of return or your ROI (Return on investment). The ROI makes your property analysis complete because it shows you what you will get from a property in comparison to what you have invested in it. The formula of ROI= cash flow/ investment.

For a property to be a good deal, it must have a reasonable ROI. By reasonable, we mean the cash flow of the property should be higher or the investment of the property lower. Below are two examples of investments that have reasonable ROI.

- **High-interest saving accounts**

High-interest savings accounts normally have a return of 5%. Mathematically, this means for every $100 you deposit in your savings account, you will get $4 in return at the end of the year. So the ROI will be 4/100 = 4%.

- **Stock market**

A stock market usually has an ROI of 8-10%, which is very impressive

Those are some of the best investments to have. So how does your property compare to them? To find out, you need to find out the ROI of your property. Here is how:

There are three ROI numbers that you need to look for in order to get the correct rate of return. Below is an exploration of the three rates.

1. **Capitalization rate (Cap rate)**

One of the most important numbers to have when doing a rental property analysis is the Cap rate of the property. This is because the cap rate is like the NOI in the sense that it is also independent of the buyer and his financing details. So it gives you the ideal indication of what your property will generate.

Now let's calculate the cap rate for your property.

The formula for calculating cap rate is as follows; **Cap rate = NOI/Property price.** In our property, our cap rate will be 49,489 divided by 520,00 which equals to 9.51%. The cap rate is like the return on investment that you would have got if you paid for the property in cash.

So what is the ideal cap rate that will show you the property is a good deal?

The answer to that question highly depends on the area that you are looking to invest in. If the average Cap Rate in the area you are in is 12%, then your ideal Cap Rate should be 12% or greater. Getting a property with a Cap Rate below 12% is not a good deal because similar properties are getting higher returns on the same area that you are in. But generally, any property in an area with an average Cap Rate of 8-12% range is a good deal. And as you can see, the ROI of your property is higher than the savings account and stock market.

Cash-On-cash Return (COC)

The truth is, not everyone can afford to pay for a property in cash. In fact, the majority of investors in real estate don't. What they do is they get loans to finance their real estate investments. This means that although the Cap rate is an important analysis, it only applies to investors who buy their rental properties using cash.

So what happens to the investors who depend on loans? We do a return on investment analysis called the cash-on-cash return. The same way we have multiple measures of income with NOI, which is completely independent of financial details and Cash Flow, which is dependent on financial details is the same way we have multiple measures of return; in Cap Rate, which is an independent rate of return and the Cash-On-Cash return, which is dependent of financial details. In short, COC is a customized way of knowing the rate of return you will get in a property as it takes into account the amount of cash you have put down on the investment.

How to calculate the COC;

Cash-On-Cash is equal to Cash flow divided by Investment Basis. In our property, the cash flow was $17,797 and our investment amounted to $120,000 meaning our COC is 17,797/120,000= 14.83%. As you can see, the return that you will get when your finance is taken into account is greater than the stock market and savings account which means that the 10-unit complex is a good deal. Basically, any investment that has a 10% and above on return is a good deal. That said, you shouldn't make a decision based on only the Cash-On-Cash return as there are other considerations that affect your bottom line, which you will look at in your third ROI number.

Total ROI

When analyzing a property, it is important to look at the total ROI because unlike COC, it actually takes into account all the financial considerations that affect the bottom line of your property's performance. Some of the property considerations that it takes into account include equity Accrued, property appreciation, and tax consequences.

The total ROI is calculated in the following way; **Total ROI= Total return/Investment basis.**

The total return is based on taxes, appreciation, equity accrual, and Cash Flow. So how do we calculate the total return of our property? To do that, you must have the figures of the aforementioned factors but since we don't have them, we are going to assume as following;

- There are no tax breaks for our property
- The equity accrued in the first year of the mortgage is $3,500
- There will be a 2% appreciation on the value of the property. This will be $10,000

So the total return of our property will be 17,797 + 3,500 +10,000 + 0 = 31,297. The total ROI will then be 31,297 divides by 120,000= 26%

Having a total ROI of 26% is a very good deal (actually better than what most investments give on return).

The above is everything you need to know to analyze a rental property to see if it's worth your investment or not.

That said, you should know that the analysis we have just done only stands true for the first year of ownership of the property. In the subsequent years, the percentage will change because a lot of factors like your tax situation, rental rates, expenses on the property and accrued annual equity might change hence causing either an increase or decrease in your ROI assessment. So the best thing for you to do when assessing a property is to extend your analysis for a couple of years. You can do that by using the demographic and trend data to calculate the ROI of your investment in future years.

So how do you evaluate a real estate wholesale deal? Learn that in the chapter below.

Evaluating A Real Estate Wholesaling Deal

As you saw above, real estate wholesaling is one of the popular strategies that one can use especially a beginner to get started in real estate. Why? The number one reason why real estate wholesaling is such a good strategy for beginners is that it requires little or no capital to start. The second reason why this method is so popular is that with it, you don't need to own a property or even renovate it to make money.

So How Does Real Estate Wholesaling Work?

Real estate wholesaling normally involves three parties; the seller, the mediator who is the wholesaler and the buyer.

Basically, what happens is a wholesaler looks for properties that are under market value (selling for less than the properties on the same block for whatever the reason might be) and then negotiate a deal with the seller to pay a certain amount of money for the property. The wholesaler and the buyer then sign a contract that says the wholesaler or anyone who he sells the contract to can buy the property for the agreed price within a certain duration of time which can be anywhere between 15-30 days. The wholesaler then looks for a buyer who he/she can sell the property to and earn a wholesaler fee or an assignment fee before the contract expires.

Why do buyers use a wholesaler to acquire property?

On the surface, it doesn't make sense why a person can buy a property from a wholesaler and end up paying more money than he/she would have if they searched for the property themselves. But it makes perfect sense because a lot of buyers, especially flippers, are way too busy working on the projects they have to spare some time to find new deals. Therefore, it is convenient for them to use a wholesaler to find new deals and that's why wholesaling is a marketable field.

So how do you know if a wholesaling deal is good or not?

To know whether a wholesaling deal is good or not, you must evaluate the deal to see if it's viable or not. Here is a step by step method on how you can evaluate a wholesale property;

Step 1: Gather Information

The first step to evaluate a wholesaling property is to gather as much information as possible about the real estate deal. What information should you be looking for, specifically? Well, you should ideally look for:

1: Sellers information

The first set of information you should gather is the information about the owner of the property. In wholesaling you normally sign a contract with the seller so it's extremely important for you to know their name, their phone number, and email for communication purpose.

2: Realtor's information

In wholesaling, you will not always have to deal with the owner of the property. There are times you will be dealing with real estate agents that the seller assigned his/her property to. So in case you are dealing with a real estate agent, you need to take their contact information like their phone numbers, email address and not forgetting their names. If you also have a realtor helping you find a deal, you should also have their contacts.

3: Property information

This is one of the most important information to gather if it's not the most information to gather. Gathering the property information is vital because it determines your success or failure in real estate. As an investor, you need to collect all the possible information that you can get about the property that you are evaluating. Find out:

- ✓ What is the address of the property?
- ✓ What size is the property
- ✓ How many bedrooms and bathrooms does the property have
- ✓ Does the property have any special features?

- ✓ What type is the property? Is it a commercial, multifamily or single-family property
- ✓ What amenities does the property have?

Some of the above questions can be answered by the seller but you shouldn't rely on their word. Counter check the information by either visiting the property or compare the property information against the property card online.

4: The properties condition

The condition of a real estate property usually makes a lot of difference when it comes to how the property is valued and how the property is sold. Therefore, it is important for you to check the condition of a property you are interested in. The first thing that you should check is the repair needs of the property. Record the amount of repair that the property needs as you try and uncover whether the property has been repaired recently or not. This information will help you a lot when calculating if a property is a good deal or not.

5: Listing information

Some real estate properties are usually sold by the owners themselves but a good number of them are listed with real estate agents who negotiate the property on behalf of the seller. So one of the things you must find out about the property you are interested in is whether the property is listed with a real estate agent or not. If it is, then you will need to gather the listing information. Find out:

- ✓ When the listing expires
- ✓ Has the property received any offers yet? If yes, what was the offer and why was it rejected by the seller
- ✓ Has the listing price reduced?
- ✓ How long has the property been listed?
- ✓ What is the name and contacts of the real estate agent?

6: The seller's motivation

For you to get a great deal, the seller has to be motivated to sell the property. Sellers who are unmotivated or lack the urgency to sell their property are usually a waste of your time because they usually don't allow you to renegotiate their asking price and some of the asking prices are normally very high. So before you even think of going to the table with a seller or a realtor, it is important for you to learn the level of urgency or motivation that a seller has. You can do that by asking smart questions to the seller like;

- ✓ Why do you want to sell the property and why this time?
- ✓ How quickly do you want to sell the property?
- ✓ What is your ideal closing date?
- ✓ If your property doesn't sell, what will be your alternative?

The above information is very important when it comes to analyzing a real estate wholesaling deal. It helps you identify which deals to walk away from and which deals are good for you.

Step 2: Do Some Wholesaling Mathematics

Mathematics is not everyone's cup of tea but you must do it if you are to be a successful real estate wholesaler. That said, the math that you will be doing when evaluating a wholesale deal is not that hard. In fact, it is pretty easy once you get the hang of it.

So the second step that you are going to take is doing some maths and see whether the property you are looking at is worth your time or not. Here is how:

As a wholesaler, your work is normally to find deals for other people and earn a wholesaler's fee. So for you to know if a property can earn you a fee or not, you need to first find out what you need to pay for the property and the only way to do that is to start your math calculations at the end and work your way backward. Why? For a wholesale deal to be profitable to you, it must take the following factors into account;

- **The buyer's profit**: For you to sell a property to a flipper, you need to consider his profit or else they won't find any benefit in buying the property from you.

- **The property repair cost**: This is how much it will take to fix the property up

- **The wholesale profit**: The amount you want to make from the deal

- **Fixed costs**. This is the amount of money that is going to cost the flipper which includes transaction and holding costs

So How Do You Go About Calculating A Wholesale Deal?

Calculating a wholesale deal usually involves you calculating the amount you will end up paying for the property, known as the Maximum Allowable Offer (MAO). This is the amount that you can offer a seller and still be able to make some profit. As you have just learned, to get the MAO, you need to start your calculation backward. Here is the formula:

MAO = ARV – Flipper's/buyers profit – Repair cost – Fixed costs – Wholesale fee

The above step showed you how to come up with the **repair costs** but if you find it difficult, you can hire an investigator that will help you come up with the amount the property will need to be fixed up.

To find the flippers profit price, you will need to research and see how much the flippers you know and you are intending to sell the property to are comfortable taking home as profit. Is it $25,000, $30,000 or $35,000? Find out and indicate.

The **wholesale fee** is the amount of profit that you will want to get out of the deal. So think and come up with it.

To determine the **fixed costs,** you must do some due diligence and find out how much holding and transaction costs that the buyer will incur. An estimate of holding costs for a period of 4 months when the property will be undergoing renovation is good. Add the taxes, utility fee, loan fees, and any other expenses. Add the holding fee with the closing costs.

How To Come Up With The ARV

One of the most important numbers in the MAO calculation is the ARV. This is because it shows the amount that the property can be sold for after repairs and that's important because all the other figures are subtracted from it.

So how do you accurately determine a property's ARV?

Finding the ARV has one easy principle; the property is worth about what similar houses have sold for recently in your properties locale. For instance, if a house in the neighborhood sold for $ 200,000 and it has the same features as the house you are looking at, then the ARV of the property is $200,000. That said, you will not always find an identical house to compare with the property you are interested in. Sometimes you will find the closest house you can compare prices with has fewer bedrooms, land space and even bathrooms than yours so you must factor those changes when estimating the ARV.

The best way to find the ARV of a property is to consult a local real estate agent who can use their huge amount of data of sold properties to calculate the ARV price of your property and come up with a comparable market analysis (CMA). This usually comes at a small price so prepare yourself.

Below is an example of a real estate wholesale deal and how you can calculate it.

A 4 bedroom, 3 bathroom family house in Beverly Hills is on sale because the owner can't afford his payments any longer and he is facing foreclosure. Here are the details of the property;

- *The ARV for the property is $350,000*
- *The owner owes the bank $60,000*
- *The house has outstanding bills and needs that amount to $18,000*
- *The owner wants $30,000 as his walkaway money*
- *The repair price as indicated by the owner is $10,000*

For the sake of calculation, let's assume that the wholesaler's fee that you want is $5,000, the flippers profit is $30,000 and the holding cost for 6 months (time required to rehab) is $5,000.

Calculation

The first step that you are going to take when you get such a deal is to gather information about it. A lot of owners tend to underestimate their properties so that they look attractive but you need to investigate them to get the actual figures. So let's say you have investigated it and you have discovered the repair price is $ 15,000. Let's now calculate:

60,000 (the seller owes) + 18,000 (seller's bills) + 30, 000 (closing lost) = 108,000 the seller wants 108,000 + 5,000 (holding price) = 113,000

MAO=350,000(ARV) -30,000(profit term) – 15,000 (fix up) – 113,000(holding asking cost) – 5,000 fee you (163,000) =187,000

So the right price for you to pay in this deal is $187,000.

If the math is difficult for you, you can ease the process by using a wholesaling calculator which will help you identify the amount of money you need to pay for the property for it to be a good wholesaling deal. Below is one of the best calculators to use.

https://www.biggerpockets.com/wholesaling-calculator

That is how you determine whether a wholesale deal is worth investing in or not. The next step is now for you to learn how to evaluate a real estate rehabbing deal.

EVALUATING REAL ESTATE REHABBING DEAL

Real estate rehabbing is today a very popular real estate investment strategy of and this is thanks to the numerous house flipping shows on television. While these shows are very educative, they also leave out a lot of details that are important to an investor like you who wants to ensure you get a house flipping profit when you invest in this field. But don't worry; this chapter is going to educate you on how you can be an expert in-house flipping by teaching you the most important lessons which are how to tell if a real estate rehab deal is viable.

Here is a step by step method on how to evaluate a real estate rehab deal

Step 1: Learn How To Identify A Good House To Flip

Any house flipping expert who has experience in the field of rehab will tell you that you make your money when you sign the paperwork and buy the house. That is true but none of that matters if you don't know how to identify a house that has some hidden value in the first place. Below is a list of features that can help you choose the right house to consider flipping.

- ✓ **The location of the property**

When it comes to flipping, the location of the property is usually everything. This is because the location usually determines how much the house is going to sell for. The worst place to consider flipping a house is in an underprivileged neighborhood because properties in those areas sell at a very low price, which can reduce your profit significantly.

So what's the best location for you to find houses to flip?

The best location for a house flipping hunt are in good neighborhoods and the best houses to flip are the worst looking houses in that area. These deals are usually tough to find but they are the best buys because you can renovate and raise the standard of a bad looking house to meet the standard of the houses around it and then you can sell it for a good amount of money.

- ✓ **The competitiveness of the deal**

The best houses to consider for flipping are those houses that have less competition from other real estate investors. This is because competition raises a property's value and also makes it challenging for you to acquire the property since you can be outbid. All that reduces your chance of getting a good house to flip. So the best thing is for you to look for houses that are less competitive. How? By finding the most highly motivated sellers like;

- A frustrated landlord who is sick of the up and downs of renting out his/her property

- An eager bank that wants to get rid of a foreclosed house

- A family that is expecting a baby and needs to upgrade to a bigger house. These parents are usually very motivated to sell their house.

- People who have been given job transfers. These lot usually don't have much time to sell their house, which makes them very motivated.

The trick here is to keep an eye on the highly motivated sellers, approach them and make them feel like you are their only way out, which automatically gets rid of competition, as they won't go anywhere else.

✓ **Available social amenities**

A lot of house flips are normally bought by first-time homebuyers and one of the things that are common about new homebuyers is they are a young couple who either have small kids or they have kids on the way. This means the best places to look for houses to flip are places that have social amenities that young couples might need like good schools, hospitals, and public parks.

✓ **Structural problems**

As a flipper, your work is usually to fix a broken house and sell it. Therefore, one of the key things that you should look at when looking for a house to flip is the extent of the repair in a house.

Fixing some peeling paint, broken windows, broken doors and revamping a driveway is an okay task to take on as a house flipper but what is not is fixing a house with major structural problems. First of all, it will force you to rebuild the house which will take you months, which is a very long period for a flip and second, it will be a very costly fix that will reduce your profit margin if any. So look for the houses that don't have major structural problems.

Now that you know what to look for when you want to have a profitable flip, you should bear in mind that you can't purchase a house solely based on the features you have just seen. You also have to do some maths and see if a property is profitable and how profitable can it be before you even sign the papers and buy the property. The subsequent steps will show you how and what calculations you should do when evaluating a deal.

Step 2: Determine the ARV (After Repaired Value)

As you may now know, the ARV is what the property you are looking into will be worth once it has been fixed. Just like in real estate wholesaling, we use a bottom-up approach when calculating the viability of a flipping house, which means the first thing that you are going to figure out is the ARV so that you can know the end selling price of the house to know whether there will be any room for profits. If you don't know the ARV, then you will have no place to work back from.

So how do you determine the ARV?

To figure out the ARV, you will have to look at the comps or comparables, which are houses that have recently sold or are up for sale and are similar to the subject property. The comps normally determine the house's going rate and are a good estimation of what your house will be selling for.

Basically, there are two approaches through which you can determine the ARV of the subject property.

- ✓ *By visiting comparable property sites*

To calculate the ARV, you need to access comparable properties data and one way to do that is by visiting paid or free service sites like:

www.redfin.com

www.zillow.com

Once you visit the above sites, you can look at houses that fall under the following criteria:

- ✓ They are in a similar neighborhood with the subject property
- ✓ They are close in age, bed/bath count, square footage and size with the subject house
- ✓ They are located within ½-3/4 miles of the subject house
- ✓ They were sold in the last 90-120 days.

By looking at these houses and their selling prices, you will be able to get an idea of what the selling price of your house can be. For instance, if 4 houses similar to the subject house sold for $100,000, $120,000, $110,000 and $115,000, then the after repair value for the subject house can comfortably be $110,000.

- ✓ **Through a real estate agent**

The best way that you can use to come up with an accurate after repair value of a subject property is by assigning the task to your realtor or real estate agent.

Why is this approach the best way to go when you want to determine the ARV for a property? It's the best way to go because realtors run sales comparable using MLS (Multiple listing services), which only licensed agents have access to. MLS provides detailed information on all the properties that are up for sale and have recently sold. This information helps realtors to compare the market price for the property and come up with a good ARV.

Once you determine the ARV of a subject property, the next step is for you to estimate the expenses.

Step 3: Approximate The Repair Cost

The third step that you need to take is to estimate the cost of repair for the subject house. The cost of repair is an important estimate to do because it is one of the expenses that must be factored when you are calculating if a flipping deal can offer you the profit you desire.

The best way to determine the repair cost of a subject house is to hire a licensed contractor who can inspect the house and tell you just how much you will need to repair the house.

That said, if you don't want to pay for an inspector, you can use the **'$20 per square feet' rule**.

The $20 per square feet rule refers to a guideline that helps you estimate what the property you are interested in is going to cost to fix up. This rule comes from experience which dictates that houses require a full standard cosmetic rehab cost of $20 per square foot. This means that a house that is around 1,200 sq. ft. can cost (1,200 x $20) $24,000 in rehab. That said, the standard cosmetic rehab cost of $20 per sq. ft. only includes a little bit of landscaping, blinds and window treatments, new bathrooms/kitchen appliances (like appliances, granite, and cabinets), doors, electrical, baseboards and plumbing fixtures, inside and outside paints and new carpet and hard surface flooring. This rule basically assumes you are rehabbing a mid or entry type of house.

So if you want the method to work for the property you are inspecting, you will have to either increase or decrease the price of this rule. For instance, if the subject property is a high-end house that uses high-quality materials, you can adjust the rate to either $25 or $30 per sq. ft. If there are any additional needs to rehab the property, you will just add them to the estimate. For instance, if you need a new pool that will cost $6,000 and the subject house is 1,200 sq. ft. you will need to add $5,000 to $24,000 (the standard rehab cost) to get $29,000. On the other hand, if the subject house doesn't need the fix-ups that have been factored on the standard cosmetic rehab estimate of $20, you can remove the price of that particular item from the rehab cost. For instance, if all you need to fix up in a house is to refurbish the kitchen because the house has a new paint and carpet, then you can redo the house for as little as $24,000 - $15,000 = $9,000. That's basically how you can estimate the repair price yourself. At first, the method might be difficult but you will get better with time.

Step 4: Calculate the Holding and Closing Expenses

When calculating an offer or whether a flipping property is worth your time, you need to be aware of the holding and closing costs. These costs normally affect the overall amount of money that you can make from a deal so it's important for you to know how much they are in the first place.

✓ Purchasing Costs

The purchasing closing costs refer to the expenses that you incur when you buy a house. Normally, the seller pays for many of the purchasing closing costs. However, one of the purchasing costs that you are going to incur is the 0.5% of the purchase price when buying a house. So if you bought a house for $100,000 then your purchasing cost will be $500.

✓ Selling closing costs

As you have now learned, the selling closing costs are a little bit more than the purchasing costs you will incur when buying a property. So what are the selling closing costs you should expect to have?

First of all, if you use an agent when selling a property, you usually have to pay them a commission of 5-6%. So if you sold the property for $100,000 and the agent wants 5%, you will have to pay them $5,000. Secondly, you have to set aside at least 1% of the selling price to cover additional closing costs like attorney fees, escrow or title. This means you will have to pay an additional $1,000. Lastly, some buyers can ask for concessions that will help them pay for their expenses but this is dependent on the area and market you are in. Concessions can range from 1%-6%. This means your closing cost can go up to 10% of the price of the property, which can be $10,000 if you sold a house for $100,000.

✓ Holding costs

Holding costs are the expenses that you incur during the period when you are fixing up a house to resell. Some of the holding costs include maintenance cost, utility cost, insurance cost, and property tax. You will need to research and see how much these expenses will be and then add them together.

✓ Financing cost

This cost normally applies to you if you use borrowed money to finance your flip. Below are the percentages that you can expect to pay when you borrow money from lenders.

- **Hard money lenders** will ask for 12% annually and might ask for additional fees. The best thing is to estimate up to 1% additional fees. So if you borrow from a hard money lender $100,000 and you are paying 24% annually, you will calculate what percent you are paying each month which is 24 divided by 12 to make 2%. That will translate to $2,000 per month. Then you will add the additional cost which is 1% each month. That equals $1,000. If you hold the property for 4 months, you will pay $3,000 x 4 = $12,000

- **Private money lenders** normally ask for 8-12% annual return. So if you took a $100,000 loan and you hold the property for 5 months, it means you will pay the lender 1% (12 divided by 12 to get what percent you will be paying per month), which is $1,000 x 5 (the number of months you will be holding the property) = $5,000

Step 5: Determine Your Profit Expectation

The fifth step is for you to factor in the amount of money you would expect as profit. This step is important because the purpose of you flipping is so that you can earn some profit and not just any profit but the kind that is worth your time. For instance, it is hard for you to flip a house that will give you $5,000 when you can make a profit of $20,000 by flipping another property elsewhere. The ideal profit to have when flipping a house is somewhere between 10%-15%.

Sit down with yourself and come up with a number that you will be happy with as profit.

Step 7: Calculate Your Offer

Now that you know the ARV of the property, you are looking into and all expenses it can incur, the final step is for you to calculate an offer.

The formula for coming up with an offer price is:

Offer = ARV - Repair cost – Holding and closing cost – Desired profit

Let us now look at an example and calculate its offer.

You own a 4,000sq. ft. and you want to sell it for a profit of $44,000.

The after repair value is %440,000

Calculation

Repair cost; $20 x 2,000 = $40,000

Closing and holding cost; 3% private money financing + 1% (holding cost) + 1% purchasing close + 8% (selling cost) = $24,000

Main calculation; 440,000 – 24,000 – 40,000 – 44,000 = 332,000. The offer price on the above example will need to be $332,000 for it to be a worthwhile deal.

That's how you evaluate a real estate rehabbing the property.

Conclusion

We have come to the end of the book. Thank you for reading and congratulations on reading until the end.

I truly hope you found the book helpful in your quest towards finding great real estate deals that you want to close before anyone else does. The truth is; when it comes to investing in real estate, anyone can be successful. What we all need is to practice how to tell a good real estate deal from a bad one by following the instructions in this book.

If you found the book valuable, can you recommend it to others? One way to do that is to post a review on Amazon.

Thank you and good luck!

Get Your Free Copy of

How to be a Real Estate Millionaire

To Get Your Free Copy, Open the Link

https://ebraveboy_3ee2.gr8.com/

www.ingramcontent.com/pod-product-compliance
Lightning Source LLC
Chambersburg PA
CBHW052338220526
45472CB00001B/476